T0142514

FOR THE LOVE OF MONEY IS THE ROOT OF ALL ???

BISHOP JAMES T. JOHNSON

authorHOUSE®

AuthorHouse™
1663 Liberty Drive
Bloomington, IN 47403
www.authorhouse.com
Phone: 833-262-8899

© 2021 Bishop James T. Johnson. All rights reserved.

No part of this book may be reproduced, stored in a retrieval system, or transmitted by any means without the written permission of the author.

Published by AuthorHouse 04/15/2021

ISBN: 978-1-6655-2307-3 (sc)
ISBN: 978-1-6655-2306-6 (e)

Print information available on the last page.

Any people depicted in stock imagery provided by Getty Images are models, and such images are being used for illustrative purposes only. Certain stock imagery © Getty Images.

This book is printed on acid-free paper.

Because of the dynamic nature of the Internet, any web addresses or links contained in this book may have changed since publication and may no longer be valid. The views expressed in this work are solely those of the author and do not necessarily reflect the views of the publisher, and the publisher hereby disclaims any responsibility for them.

CONTENTS

FOREWORD

In this book, the author talks about money as if it's a human in the flesh, but that's the reality of the life that we live. This book is a conversation between the world and the people who read it. It defines the beauty that God has given us to work with on this earth. Money is our second provider on this earth, and you cannot take money too lightly because if you do, it will walk away from you. This book sums up how important that money really is to us in our lives. If anyone else tells you different, then their teaching about money is not correct. Allow this book to be your stepping stone to the doors opening up for you on your journey of money success in your life.

This book is a masterpiece in explaining, how, where, when, and what regarding the mastery and psychology of money. It breaks down why you are not successful financially, and why you are successful financially. It speaks on the God-given law of attraction. It is your legal right to be successful in everything that you put your mind to. You are your best or worst friend, so be good to yourself.

CHAPTER 1

IN THE BEGINNING

In the beginning God created the heaven and the earth. And the earth was without form and void; and darkness Was upon the face of the deep. And the spirit of god moved upon the face of the waters. and god said let there be light and there was light. And god saw the light, that it was good; and god divided the light from the darkness. And god called the light day, and the darkness he called night. And the evening and the morning were the first day.

—Genesis 1:1–5

This is how things got started, and we have come a long ways since the beginning. God put money here so we could use it as a bargaining chip for the exchange of goods from one person to another. Money is a gift from God for us to have and appreciate. Some people have a lot of money; some people have very little. Believe me when I tell you that without lots of money, your life can be and will be very miserable. But with it, your life will be very good—financially, anyway. We know that money does not solve all our issues, but it sure does make things a lot better when it comes to living conditions.

God knew exactly what he was doing when he created money for the exchange of goods. Some people are good at accessing it, but some people are not, and they will suffer for a very long time if they don't learn how to access it. Money is one of the very important things that God has given us. Some people really do believe that money is evil, but in fact money is your most important lifeline after God himself. Money is a perfect form that was put on this earth for humans to use to their advantage.

You need to stop making bad remarks about money. Money is like a classy lady who needs to be spoken to very gently and treated kindly. Chivalry is not dead when it comes to women (God bless). Let money be the apple of your eye, because if it is not, then you have made an enemy of money. Remember that you are not the only one who depends on money—your family does as well, and their well-being is

at stake. Make sure that you speak about money with love, because money loves you back.

Money is as kind to you as you are to it, so don't blow it. It is your best friend after God. Remember that in the beginning, there was nothing formed or shaped, but then God moved upon the earth with his mighty hand. Everything took perfect form, and that includes money. Have you heard the expression "A mind is a terrible thing to waste"? Well, listen to this expression, because he who holds the gold holds other people's happiness. Money is not a myth; it is a big reality to people who love it and understand it. Stay prayed up and paid up.

CHAPTER 2

MONEY WAS BORN

The first paper money in the United States was issued on March 10, 1862. The five-, ten-, and twenty-dollar bills issued were made legal tender by an act of Congress on March 17, 1862. Before this, people all over the world used something called the barter system, which is where people traded goods. That went on for centuries until paper money, or legal tender, showed up on the scene.

No one knows for sure who first invented such money, but historians believed metal objects were first used as money as early as 5000 BC. Around 700 BC, the Lydians became the first Western culture to make coins. Other countries and civilizations soon began to mint their own coins with specific values. Before that, the Chinese used leather notes made of one-foot square pieces of white deerskin with

colorful borders for money. The Song Dynasty was the first to issue real paper money in 1023, and the most famous Chinese issuer was Kublai Khan, a thirteenth-century Mongol leader.

The word *rupee* is from the Sanskrit word *rupya*, which means "shaped stamped, impressed, or coined," and from the Sanskrit word *raupya*, which means "silver." The rupee that we keep in our pockets today has a long and perplexing past that began in ancient India in the sixth century BC. In the nineteenth century AD, the British introduced paper money to the subcontinent. The Paper Currency Act of 1861 gave the British government the monopoly on notes issued throughout the vast expanse of British India. This was how money was born.

Even today, money is still being born. We have debit cards, we have credit cards, and we have checks. We have many ways to get money into our hands: Western Union, MoneyGram, PayPal, and ATMs. There are many more ways that I probably missed, but you get the picture. Money is being born all the time and is always at our fingertips. God did not leave us without ways to get money.

Money is the reason why we work, and it is the reason why people do a lot of things that they do. In this earthly realm, you can try to live without it all you want, but you will fail in a very miserable way. I know some people now who despise money, and if that makes you feel good, then that's your own personal problem. I myself think that people

who hate money are very lost and lonely, and their lives will be very hard because they have been brainwashed by some poor, broke person. But if you need me to wake you up and educate you on the will of God and beautiful money, I will—and I can do it very well.

You should know that when you were born, someone had to pay someone else to deliver you into this world, whether it was a government system or your mom or dad's insurance from their job. Someone had to use money to get you out of the womb of your mother. It was taken care of before you even came into this world, my lovely friend. Even Christ was born into this world once upon a time, so being born is not something that is wrong. Childbirth is good because it gives us people who will bless us for generations to come.

CHAPTER 3

FOR THE LOVE OF MONEY

How many of you reading this book right now are in a relationship with someone whom you're in love with? If you are love with someone, you will do anything for that person. But on the other hand, if you are not in love with a person and simply like that person's company, then if the person were to go to jail or have some freak accident, you would probably give a response, but you wouldn't bend over backward to help. This is the point that I'm proving to you about money.

John 3:16 says, "For God so Loved the world, that he gave his only begotten son, that whosoever believeth in him should not perish, but have everlasting life." If you don't

love something, you will not do a good job caring for it. If you have been taught all your life that money was bad, that God did not care for people with money, and that people with money are evil and of the devil, then you will not do a good job caring for your money. The belief that money is bad is a lie from hell, because money is a big tool that God has given us to help us survive. It's okay to love money and make money your best friend.

The haters of money are people who do not have much of it or who have been in poverty their entire lives. They are the Nazis behind the hating of money. Have you heard the expression "Money makes the world go around"? Or "Money talks; the rest walk"? The reason that they are walking is because they don't have any money. I decree it right now: I love money, and it loves me back. I am married to money. Money fulfills all my material needs. In some cases, money can even buy you love. I can see you laughing with me right now. Some of you will identify with me on this touchy subject and say that I'm a genius. Now. repeat after me: "I love money, and it loves me back all day and night long."

Money is a diamond that shines and sparkles twenty-four hours a day. I am encouraged by God to get money because God put money here for me and you, even if you're not a believer in money. Money is the root of all evil for people who put it before God and think that money is more important than God. Of course, those people are born fools.

Money is the reason that you labor so hard or, if you know how to master it, the reason that you have it so easy. Money is an equal partner with you. You share all your material possessions with your money. I am not afraid to say that I love money more than the haters hate money. If people tell you that they don't want to be rich, pay them no mind whatsoever; their hatred is the product of their disbelief. It's like the devil has possessed their minds and turned them against money, and now they're taking it out on money and the people who have money. Most rich people catch hell from poor folks because they're very wealthy. I guess the poor sometimes forget that someone has to be rich, because God uses the rich to supply jobs for the poor and the poor-minded. I hope this book changes your mind about loving money. Stop listening and hanging around people with a poor mentality about money. Even if they are churchgoing saints, they are the ones who may tell you that money is not important and that God said come as you are. What they are really telling you is that it's okay to be poor and dumb about the education part of money, but in fact it only hurts you for generations to come. Therefore, please love money and educate yourself about money.

CHAPTER 4

GOD, THEN MONEY, THEN FAMILY

God the Creator is always first in our lives. He created us, and we are to worship him love him, respect him, and obey his will. Nothing will go right for you until you put Christ first in your life. You must know your boundary in life with God and the people that you deal with every day. Anybody who does not respect the Creator of the world is a very dangerous person, and you should distance yourself from that person. Nothing can be obtained in life without the Creator. This entire book is dedicated to money because she is as fine as may wine. You must treat her like a lady. No matter where you are, money is divine wine that connects every vine to the tree. Without money, you cannot have a

successful family or happiness in your marriage. Money is the bandage that holds everything together in marriage and any other relationship that you have. Money guarantees materialistic happiness—why do you think they call people gold diggers? Because they know that it's no fun without money in life.

Now, I am not telling you to steal, kill, or do anything illegal for money because that's not what God wants from us. Money is not worth you losing your freedom, but it is worth fighting for in a very good way. Let money be your fuel and your guideline for you to strive for more. Trust me, your spouse will love you for it. Would you rather be on welfare or have money to support yourself and your family so your kids will proudly say, "That's my rich parent," and they want everybody to hear them as they brag about their parents' achievements? Once again, you will never be totally happy without money in your corner as a backup element. The song says money make the world go around, and the people who don't have money when the world goes around are the only ones who get dizzy. For those of you who say you love your family, but you don't have a love for money, you will not be doing your family justice in hating your brother named money. It is your parents' fault for not teaching you about the function of money and the great system of money. Even your government doesn't want you to know about the function of money. They want you dumb and ignorant about money. They want you to depend on

them for money so that they can control you even more than they do today.

I am not the creator of money, but I am one of the masters of money, and I always will be. Money and I fit like a glove, like a car to tires, and like peanut butter and jelly. We fit like white on rice, like ham on burger, and like french to fry. We fit like mama and daddy, and we fit like the rich to the rich. Don't be afraid of getting rich, and don't be afraid of rich, successful people. God has no problem with you having a ton of money. You have been trained against success, you been trained against yourself, you have been trained against your family, and you don't even recognize it. You are an enemy of life itself. Your mind is like a bottomless pit, and you're a bulldog against people who have a lot of material possessions. Trust me, your family will love you even more when you can provide them with all the material possessions they want. Money is not your enemy, no matter how you label it. Money allows your children to wear expensive clothes instead of cheap ones that shrink after you wash them in in your cheap washer and dryer set.

Right about now, you should be angry at the devil in hell and at the people who raised you and told you that money doesn't matter and is the root of all evil. Yet the people who told you that went to work every month of their lives to make minimum wage at a job where someone else told them when to show up and when to go home, like a puppet, and the entire time they were mad as hell at the

boss telling everybody what to do. They hoped the owner would burn in hell get what was coming to them. They were always quoting things like "God don't like ugly" and "those people are going to get theirs." They hate the same people who employ you so you can halfway feed your family. It's all propaganda, and you're talking trash against the hand that feeds you. That's not a good move—it's a stupid move. You're broke and angry, cursing everybody out for no reason, and all because you hate your job. You hate that you're broke, and you hate everyone who is prospering in life. You are a jealous person—and don't forget you're broke as well. You get off on being broke because you are a drama master; you love to have anyone to blame but yourself. All you have to do is look into the mirror, and then you will see who is to blame: Mr. or Mrs. Broke Pockets.

Remember this: God is first, then family. You can say all day long and all night long that you love God, but truth be told, you really don't even care for yourself because you believe that money is not useful for your life. You need to acknowledge your weakness in your life: you are really afraid of success. I hear people say that if they had money, they would give it away to other people as if money has no value, and then they would continue to go to work like nothing is wrong in their lives. You want people to look up to you and like you, so you think giving away all your money will help. What you did not consider is the fact that you will grow old.

Hopefully you won't die in the process of working hard for somebody else.

This book is a letter. It's not just chapters—it's a money masterpiece to wake you up to the reality of who God intended you to be: someone who is very responsible in life as God is in taking care of us. Have you ever heard the expression "You are who you say you are"? Most people I know are always claiming they are broke. They say things like, "Man, I wish I had some money. One day I will have some money. If it wasn't for bad luck, I wouldn't have any luck at all." That is crazy talk. All you're doing is cursing yourself and your family. God himself cannot bless your mess. You are a victim of your own circumstances and mindset. Remember that whatever your kids see you do, they will do as well. If poverty is your decision, then so be it, but you do not have to bring your kids to the gutter with you and then say to people, "Aw, but money is not the only thing in the world." This is where you're wrong. God and the money he created makes the world go around. That's why people kill for it, steal for it, and they lie for it all day long. Look at your government and how they lie to people all the time, especially politicians who want what they want and ignore you. Presidents all over the world and in every country lie over and over again, stealing money from the poor people like hotcakes out of a box. Nobody respects a liar, so the question is how you can look at yourself in the eye given the way you lie to yourself about money. No

respectable woman wants a broke man who doesn't own a thing in life and isn't going anywhere in life. You can fool a little girl but not a real woman. It's not about looks with a man or woman; it's about where you are going in life, your purpose, and your main goals.

Most people who are business-minded are not satisfied with one victory in life—they must have success over and over again. I found out that most successful people are very hardheaded, as I am. We won't stop or listen to other people at times because we don't like being told what to do. Now, that can be good and bad according to your goals, but at the same time, you are very misunderstood as a person, and people will say you're crazy until you succeeded. Then they will be either jealous of you or support you. Either you are somebody or you are nobody.

Don't ever forget that you should be an asset to your community and to all people, not just one race of people. Be the best to everyone. God can't bless a mess. Share your wisdom with all people.

CHAPTER 5

YOUR GOD-
GIVEN LAW OF
ATTRACTION

Scenario time. How many of you reading this have ever searched television or Facebook and seen a car that you liked? The very next day, you saw that particular car riding on the freeway or your neighborhood, in different colors. You probably thought, "Wow, I saw that car last night." Or perhaps you were thinking of someone, who then called you out of blue. That's amazing, huh? Actually it is just amazing grace that God gave to you to be able to call things into existence or think things into existence. It is your God-given right to be that powerful in this universe. The problem is that most of you don't even know you have this power from

God, to be able to control situations and make and set your own destiny. God has given us this life to enjoy.

I myself use and practice the law of attraction each day of my life, and it has been good to me. There are so many of you out there experiencing something that you call bad luck, but in reality it's you using the law of attraction against yourself. The next time you start experiencing bad luck in your life, know that you brought it on yourself via your own negative thoughts system.

This whole thing starts at home with your parents, who may or may not know anything about the law of attraction. If they don't know anything about lit, it's going to hurt you for a very long time until you learn about the law of attraction yourself. Your life is going to be a blunder for a very long time until you take the steps to learn about the power God has given you. Take it from me: you will be trying to figure out what in the hell is going on, because you're going to feel like you have died and gone to hell. You have a God-given power that allows you to think it up, and it will show up. It won't show up if you doubt or don't use what God has given you. You're going to continue to blame other people for the problems that you have created in your own bloodline, which probably has already been cursed anyway from your uneducated disbelief. So many people out there have made God a welfare God who is supposed to feel so sorry for them in their so-called dying needs. When it comes to money, they fall short. They feel that God is

supposed to come to their rescue when they can't pay their bills. God is supposed to come off his thrown again, hold their hands, walk with them to the bill collector's office, and hand them a check! Think this at your own risk, because God has left you with all the tools that you need to survive. People who do more complaining than making money will never succeed in life. This world will be like you are living on another planet—and you may as well be on another planet if you are living on this earth with no money.

There will be people in your own family who will find you only as valuable as the money that you have or spend on them. Maybe you will recognize it, maybe you want it, or maybe you will be in denial of the entire situation. God created money for humans so that they could use their gifts and skills for money to help themselves and other people—not so that you can curse what God has made good, honest, and true for all of us. Have you ever heard of the phrase "crabs in a barrel"? That's who you are if you are upset with other people about the money they have earned. I have seen a lot of crabs in a barrel of all colors and creeds, running around like theirs heads are cut off like a chicken. Remember the old words from the 1990s: can't we all just get along? Being decent is sometimes just a word. In many cases, there are a lot of people out there who don't want anything out of life. They forget the proper hierarchy in life: God first, money second, family third.

CHAPTER 6

MONEY IS YOUR BEST FRIEND

Money is your best friend on this earth realm. You can't beat its loyalty because money will never betray you. Money will never gossip about you behind your back. Money will never leave you as long as you treat it right and say good things about it. It will do whatever you need it to do in its God-given power to aid you with whatever you need. Money can do just about all things in this world that you need it to do. You simply have to trust in God that he will deliver it to you so you can have enough to bless others as well. Money has feelings and knows when a person speaks bad or good about it. Money is a woman who has strong feelings about what you say about her and how you treat her.

Have you ever heard the song by the great Motown group the Temptations? They wrote a song called "Treat Her Like a Lady." Of course they were speaking of a woman, but it also falls into the category of money. Yes, people, money is your best friend. No matter how you try to write her off, she will never die and will keep multiplying like the grass that grows in the summer months. Money is like a very expensive bottle of wine. Money is like a diamond ring on your finger. Money is the boss over many people and things. Money is the love of your life, and if you let her be, she will never make you cry unless you don't have enough of her. Then she will make you cry like a newborn baby just being born. Money is the sunshine on the earth. Money is the muff, as a close friend of mine words it. Money is the stamina in your life. Money is that pot of gold at the end of the rainbow.

I know that right now, somebody who is reading this masterpiece on money is hating on this book because they do not have strong access to the money. Money has caused people who do not understand the function of it to do evil things for it, and it is not the will of God for his people to do evil things for money. God does not honor people who will hurt others for the sake of money. Have you ever smelled the scent of money fresh off the press from being printed? It smells like magic, and we all understand that magic is amazing. Have you ever thought about your leadership in this country, which is your government? They hold all the money, and when a disaster hits our country, no matter what state its in, the

government will aid the people with money to help them out of a crisis. The first thing that we all say when it happens is, "Will the government step in and help us out?" You see, that's money you're talking about not, food stamps, even though the government does help out with that form of money assistance.

As you can tell, money is a big factor in our lives today, tomorrow, and every day after that. We and money are one forever, because the earth realm has a need for a buy-and-trade system. Now how do you like those apples and oranges? And b\y the way, apples and oranges cost money as well. You can't name too many things on this earth that don't cost money.

There are some people who sell their souls to the devil for money. When it gets to be that serious that you will sell your soul to the devil, then you are in a lot of trouble, and you probably don't even care. Look at this economy that we are in right now, dealing with the COVID-19 pandemic. The economy is in bad shape. People have lost their jobs and can't support their families or pay their bills. All of this is because they don't have their best friend, money, to back them up, and we all know the government will stall as long as they can so they do not have to do anything for you. Now are you recognizing the real power of money. Business owners are crying in their sleep because their businesses have gone under. Once again, money is your best friend. Now you're trying to get it from the government. People prostitute for money, pray for money, and even fast for money. It has a stronghold that cannot be beaten or broken. The old saying is if you cannot beat them, then join them.

CHAPTER 7

FOR THE LOVE OF MONEY IS THE ROOT OF ALL BLESSINGS

— ✦ —

Yes, people, I said it. Money is the root of all blessings. You have been taught that verse from the Bible the wrong way. I cannot see God making money an evil thing. It's the way it has been taught to people that has them confused about money. Once again, money makes the world go around, and without it you wouldn't be made whole. The improper teaching about money has scared your pants and skirts off. Money is a blessing to have, and if you are able enough to have it in a large capacity, you are very blessed and do

not have to work your fingers to the bone to get it in large quantities.

You simply need to have a good mindset with it. You are the master of money—it is not the master of you. You are the boss; you are the head and not the tail. You are the father and not the child. You tell money when, where, how, and what to do at all times. You control the function of your own money. Money is the root of nearly all blessings to come true, people even call me about how they had a dream that they had lots of money or won lots of money. I simply smile, laugh, and agree with them about their dreams. If only they knew that they can manifest that money into their bank accounts. Most of them are very ignorant about the love of money because they were never taught at home that they could be very rich. They were not taught that they could own their own company. Instead, they would rather play the victim of money and beg everybody for money. They love telling people that they do not have any money so that they can be friends with the next broke person who is ignorant about money. You know the drill: two small minds think alike, because you attract to you the type of person that you are. Therefore, losers hang around with losers, and winners hang around with winners. Most of you say that you love the Lord up above, yet you do not practice what he gave you, which is called an abundant lifestyle. The main people who are going to tell you that money is the root of all evil will be those who have no money, or those who are the broke

church folk. They are looking for a handout from God himself and are ignorant of the fact that God has already left them with the abundant mindset to go out and create more money. Yes, it's true: you can think and grow rich if you exercise your belief in your power that has been given to you. Yes, it's okay to admit you love money, and it's okay to admit that money is the love of your life on this earth. It's better to make a good run for money and fail at it than to stand there and do nothing. And yes, you will fail a few times before money comes to you in its full intentions, but you will succeed eventually because when you are in practice of getting all the money that you can, it has no other choice but to obey your command. Money has ears and is not deaf at all. It hears everything that you say about it. It knows whether you are its best friend or whether you are against it, meaning you are an enemy to money. It also has feelings along with its ears. Money has superpowers like Superman. Make an enemy with money, and it will walk away from you until you understand its worth in your life and in your family's life. Money hears your good intentions and your bad intentions.

I have seen people go from rags to riches overnight. When they changed their thinking and bad talk about money, then were able to prosper, It will happen for you the same way if you change your tune about money. The love of money is the root of all your financial dreams to come true. The love of money is the root of all blessings. This

book is intended to encourage you not to praise money but to get your mindset in the understanding that having money means you can take care of yourself and your family, who deserve to be taken care of very properly.

God bless you all. May you forever prosper. Remember that money has never been an evil thing—it was simply the evil hands it was in.

ABOUT THE AUTHOR

Master Teacher Bishop James T. Johnson is a special deliverance preacher and healer, as well as a motivational speaker. He is the founder of Prophetic House of God International Ministries.

Master Teacher is fluent in preaching, teaching, and motivating people to be the best that they can be in life. He is also a mentoring life coach who can help you become someone that you have never been before.

In this book, your mind will be challenged, about everything that you have ever done in your life to get ahead of the game. Life is not a race—it's a walk through the park when you have the right wisdom from someone who is a master at what he or she does.

Master Teacher Bishop James T. Johnson
PO Box 261
Wiggins, MS 39577

www.prophetichouseofgodministries.com

Email: bishopjohnson7777@gmail.com

Printed in the United States
by Baker & Taylor Publisher Services